Keeping **Unusual** Pets

Geckos

WITHDRAWN

Sonia Hernandez-Divers

Chicago, Illinois

H **www.heinemannraintree.com**
Visit our website to find out
more information about
Heinemann-Raintree books.

To order:

☎ Phone 888-454-2279

⌨ Visit www.heinemannraintree.com
to browse our catalog and order online.

Edited by Louise Galpine, Megan Cotugno, and Laura Knowles
Designed by Kim Miracle and Victoria Bevan
Picture research by Mica Brancic
Originated by Capstone Global Library Ltd 2010
Printed and bound in China by Leo Paper Products Ltd

14 13 12 11 10
10 9 8 7 6 5 4 3 2

Library of Congress Cataloging-in-Publication Data
Hernandez-Divers, Sonia, 1969-
  Geckos / Sonia Hernandez-Divers. -- 2nd ed.
    p. cm. -- (Keeping unusual pets)
  Includes bibliographical references and index.
  ISBN 978-1-4329-3849-9 (hc)
  1. Geckos as pets--Juvenile literature. I. Title.
  SF459.G35H47 2010
  639.3'952--dc22
                        2009035277

Acknowledgments
The author and publisher are grateful to the following for permission to reproduce copyright material: Alamy p. **39 bottom** (Beanstock Images/© First Light); Ardea pp. **11** (Geoff Trinder), **9 top** (P. Morris), **29 top**; © Bruce Coleman Collection p. **33 top** (Animal Ark); © Capstone Global Library Ltd pp. **13 top**, **13 bottom**, **16**, **17**, **18 bottom**, **19**, **21 top**, **21 bottom**, **22**, **23**, **24**, **25 bottom**, **26 top**, **26 bottom**, **30**, **32**, **34 top**, **35**, **37 top**, **38**, **39 top**, **43 top**, **43 bottom**, **44 top** (Gareth Boden Photography); **45** (Trevor Clifford), **29 bottom**, **36**, **40**, **41**, **42** (Tudor Photography); © Capstone Publishers pp. **4**, **20**, **25 top**, **27**, **28**, **31 bottom**, **34 bottom**, **37 bottom**, **44 bottom** (Karon Dubke); Corbis p. **7** (Joe McDonald); FLPA p. **15 top**; NHPA pp. **8**, **10 top** (Daniel Heuclin), **6** (Hello & Van Ingen), **15 bottom**, **33 bottom** (Image Quest 3-D); OSF pp. **5** (www.photolibrary.com), **10 bottom**, **12** (www.photolibrary.com/© Michael Leach), **9 bottom** (www.photolibrary.com/© Mike Liney); Science Photo Library p. **31**; Sonia M. Hernandez-Divers p. **14**.

Cover photograph of a young leopard gecko reproduced with permission of Shutterstock (© Eric Isselée).

We would like to thank Judy Tuma for her invaluable help in the preparation of this book.

Every effort has been made to contact copyright holders of material reproduced in this book. Any omissions will be rectified in subsequent printings if notice is given to the publisher.

Contents

What Is a Gecko?..4

Gecko Facts 6

Eggs and Babies 14

Is a Gecko for You? 16

Your Gecko's Home 20

Feeding Your Gecko..24

Caring for Your Gecko..28

Handling Your Gecko 32

Common Problems 36

Visiting the Vet 40

Keeping a Record 42

Understanding Geckos..44

Glossary 46

Find Out More 47

Index 48

Any words appearing in the text in bold, **like this**, are explained in the glossary.

What Is a Gecko?

Geckos are beautiful and interesting animals. They are a lot of fun to watch and are unlike any other pet you are likely to meet! Geckos are a type of lizard, and lizards belong to a large group of animals called **reptiles**. Like other reptiles, geckos have no hair and their bodies are covered with scales. They do not make milk for their young and they are **cold-blooded**, which means they need to soak up heat from their surroundings.

A gecko has a broad head, long body, long tail, and scaly skin.

Why are geckos special?

With their broad heads and plump, long tails, geckos look different from most other lizards. Most geckos have fairly dull-colored skin that helps them to blend in with their surroundings, although some are very brightly colored. Their skin looks like tiny, bead-like scales. The skin of some geckos feels as soft as velvet!

Geckos have some special characteristics that set them apart from other lizards. Most of them have toe pads that allow them to climb very well. They are also the only type of lizard that can make noises. There are laughing geckos, barking geckos, and even singing geckos! Sometimes it is hard to believe that such small creatures can make such loud noises.

Did you know?

• Most geckos are **arboreal**, which means they spend most of their time in trees.

• They have sticky pads made up of tiny hairs on their toes that help them cling onto surfaces. Geckos can run along ceilings completely upside down!

• All geckos feed on small animals, usually insects.

• Geckos are the only type of lizard that can make noises.

• Most geckos lay eggs, but some **species** give birth to their babies.

• Some people think that geckos are poisonous, but this is not true.

Because most geckos do not have eyelids, they cannot blink to keep their eyes moist. Instead, they clean their eyes with their tongue!

STAYING SAFE

When a **predator** chases after a leopard gecko, the leopard gecko's tail can break off. The predator goes after the tail, while the lizard escapes. This **defense mechanism** protects the life of the leopard gecko. Because the supply of fat that is stored in the tail is lost, the lizard will have to eat a lot to make up for the lost energy. A new tail will grow, but it will be shaped differently from the original one.

Unlike some other gecko species, the leopard gecko cannot escape by climbing vertical (upright) surfaces. Its feet do not have the tiny hairs that cling to those surfaces. However, leopard geckos are able to climb some rough vertical surfaces to reach safety.

Gecko Facts

There are more than 800 **species** of geckos throughout the world. Because geckos depend on the sun for warmth, in the wild they are found only in warm countries. Geckos can live in a variety of **habitats**, but most of them are found in deserts, on mountains, and in tropical rain forests.

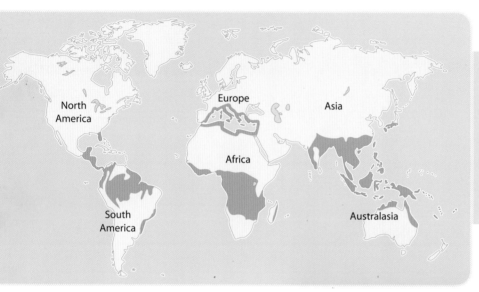

Geckos are found in all the areas colored blue. These are some of the warmest regions of Earth.

Geckos around the world

The most common gecko in Europe is the wall gecko. Wall geckos are sometimes also known as Mediterranean geckos because they are found around the Mediterranean Sea. Wall geckos spend most of their day **basking** in the sunshine. At night, they often group around porch lights to hunt for insects.

At night, geckos eat insects that are attracted to porch lights.

In the United States, the two most common wild geckos are the leaf-fingered gecko and the banded, or ground, gecko. Many other species have arrived in the United States over the last 200 years. These species have traveled in the cargoes of ships from other countries and have then settled down in warm areas such as Florida.

This western banded gecko is one of the most common types of wild gecko to be found in the United States.

Geckos under threat

Predators and habitat destruction are the two greatest threats to geckos. Among the predators are rats, weasels, and cats. Since many of these predators are active at night, the **nocturnal** and ground-dwelling geckos are especially vulnerable. Smaller predators can even follow the geckos into their hiding places.

The geckos' natural habitats are being destroyed by **urban sprawl.** Grasslands are burned, plowed up, and converted to fields for grazing livestock. Geckos mainly eat insects, but these are also disappearing because of the use of **pesticides.** The insects' own food supply is also becoming scarce.

DID YOU KNOW?

Geckos are very important to the world, since they eat tons of insects every day. In some parts of the world, they are responsible for keeping down the number of household pests, such as cockroaches and flies.

Gecko features

Geckos are usually small creatures—the smallest are only 30 millimeters (1 inch) long. But they can be as big as the Tokay gecko, which measures 35 centimeters (14 inches). Most geckos are nocturnal, which means they are mainly active at night, but a few species are **diurnal** (active during the day). Nocturnal geckos have cat-like eyes, with vertical **pupils** that expand so they can see better in the dark. Diurnal geckos usually have round pupils.

The Tokay gecko is one of the largest geckos in the world. It can be aggressive and has a painful bite!

Hungry hunters

Geckos have thick tongues that they use to hunt insects. When a gecko sees an insect, it jumps forward and grabs the insect with its tongue and then swallows it whole. Geckos can eat many insects in one sitting. Some larger geckos even eat other lizards, small shrews, and mice. Some species of geckos lick **nectar** out of flowers or eat small amounts of fruit.

NO EYELIDS?

There are two major groups of geckos. One group has eyelids and the other group does not. Most geckos belong to the group with no eyelids.

Climbing high

Geckos are great climbers. At the end of each toe they have a pad covered with tiny hairs. These hairs enable the gecko to cling to almost any surface.

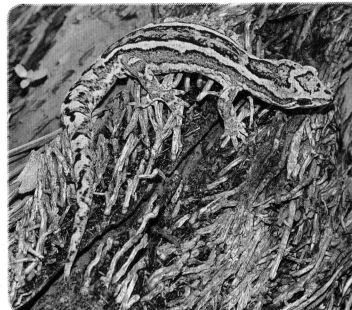

The tiny hairs on the bottom of each toe pad increase the amount of contact that the gecko's toes have with the wall. This means that a gecko can even walk on a ceiling!

Gecko colors

Some geckos have skin colors that blend in with their surroundings. This is known as **camouflage** (disguise), which allows the geckos to hide from predators. Other geckos have vivid colors. They can look very pretty, like the Phelsuma gecko, which is a beautiful green and blue color.

Gecko babies

Most geckos lay eggs, but a few species give birth to live babies. Geckos lay eggs several times a year and usually lay two eggs at a time. Once she has laid her eggs, the female gecko leaves the nest for good. Young geckos are able to care for themselves as soon as they are hatched.

The dull colors of this gecko allow it to camouflage itself against the tree trunk.

Geckos as pets

Lots of people have geckos as pets. Geckos are cool and interesting . . . but there are so many kinds to choose from!

Learn about each kind before you decide which one would be the best pet for you.

NEED TO KNOW

• Young children are not allowed to buy pets themselves. You should always have an adult with you when you buy your pet.

• Most countries have laws that say pets must be treated with respect. It is your responsibility to make sure your gecko is healthy and well cared for. Always take your pet to the vet if it is sick or injured.

The fat-tailed gecko comes from the Sahara Desert. It can be very aggressive.

The flying gecko is a large gecko that needs lots of room!

Which gecko?

Only a few species of gecko make really good pets. Some, like the Tokay gecko, should not be handled without the help of an adult because they can bite very hard. Others, like the day gecko, need special things to eat. Some geckos need special homes because they spend a lot of time climbing.

Once you have had more experience with geckos, you might be interested in owning a variety of species. But for the beginner, the best choice by far is the leopard gecko. Leopard geckos are one of the most interesting gecko species, and they are also fun and easy to own.

THE IDEAL GECKO

The ideal pet gecko should:

- not get too big
- be easy to feed
- be gentle and not aggressive.

Young leopard geckos are striped—so perhaps they should be called "tiger geckos"! As they get older, their stripes turn into spots.

Leopard geckos

The leopard gecko's scientific name is *Eublepharis macularius*. The first word means "good (or working) eyelids" because, unlike many geckos, leopard geckos have eyelids. The second word means "spotted." When leopard geckos are babies, the tops of their bodies are covered in stripes, which helps them to hide from predators by blending in with their surroundings. But as the geckos get older, their stripes shrink down to spots, so their skin looks like a leopard's skin.

Leopard gecko facts

Leopard geckos are small lizards that measure about 15 to 25 centimeters (6 to 10 inches) long. They are tan-yellow in color, with dark spots all over the top of their body. Their skin is rough and covered in growths that look like warts, but in fact these are just a kind of scale. Their bellies are plain white or tan.

GARISH GECKOS

Sometimes leopard geckos have different coloring. This is because **reptile breeders** have **bred** them to be that way. Now you can find leopard geckos that are bright yellow, or orange, or completely white.

The burrows and crevices where leopard geckos hide keep them safe from birds and other predators, but also keep them cool and moist. Otherwise, they would overheat and dry up in the desert heat!

Leopard geckos in the wild

Leopard geckos live in the rocky deserts and grasslands of Asia, India, Pakistan, Afghanistan, Iran, and Iraq—all areas where it gets really hot. There, they spend most of the day sleeping and hiding in **crevices** in rocks or in burrows. They keep hidden to avoid the heat of the day, but also to stay safe from the birds and other animals that might eat them.

At night, the geckos come out of their burrows or crevices to hunt. They walk along the ground in search of food, or sit and wait until a small insect comes by. Then they jump forward and catch it with their mouth. In the wild, leopard geckos eat a variety of insects, including scorpions! They also eat other small lizards.

Leopard geckos' toes are pointed and more like those of other lizards.

LEOPARD GECKOS ARE DIFFERENT

Leopard geckos are one of the most interesting species of gecko. Unlike most other geckos:

✪ They rarely make any noise.

✪ They have eyelids.

✪ They do not have toe pads that allow other geckos to cling to surfaces. This means there is less chance they will escape!

Leopard geckos belong to a small group of geckos that have eyelids. This means they can close their eyes when they sleep.

Eggs and Babies

By the time they are two years old, most leopard geckos are old enough to **breed**. In the wild, one male leopard gecko lives close to several females. The breeding season starts when the days become shorter and the nights become cooler.

Mating

When a male leopard gecko is ready to mate, he shows off to a female by vibrating his tail. If the female decides that the male is good enough, she will let him bite her on the neck. He then mates with her. After four to six weeks, the female starts to look pregnant. She becomes bigger, and pale bulges appear on her belly.

The sex of the baby geckos will depend on the temperature of the nest the eggs have been laid in.

HOT OR COLD?

The temperature of the nest where a gecko lays her eggs makes a difference in the sex of her babies. If the nest is in a really hot area, male baby geckos are born, but if it is cooler, most of the babies will be females.

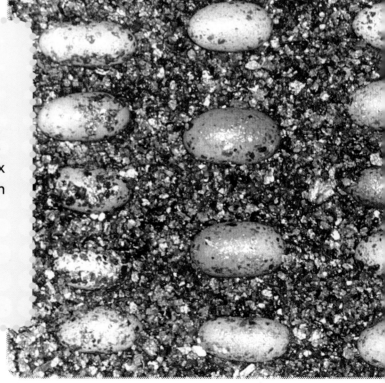

Laying eggs

When she is about six weeks pregnant, the female gecko starts to look for a warm, moist place to lay her eggs. In the wild, females dig burrows where they lay their eggs. Leopard geckos usually lay one or two eggs at a time, and a single female may lay up to six times in one season. Leopard gecko eggs take around six to eight weeks to hatch.

This baby leopard gecko has just hatched.

Baby leopard geckos

Baby leopard geckos only measure 70 to 80 millimeters (about 3 inches) in length. Once the young geckos hatch, they are able to run as well as an adult. They need to run fast in the wild, because they can easily become someone's meal if they are not careful! For the first week they do not eat anything, but after that they quickly become skilled hunters.

This young gecko is just beginning to develop its adult spots.

Is a Gecko for You?

Leopard geckos were one of the first lizards to be bred in **captivity** in large numbers. Now they are so popular that thousands are **bred** every year. Leopard geckos can make great pets, but before you buy one, you should think about some of the good and not-so-good points of owning geckos.

Leopard geckos are tiny. Even when they are fully grown, they are still small enough to hold in your hand.

GOOD POINTS

✪ Leopard geckos can be found in many pet stores, so they are much easier to buy than most other **species**.

✪ They are not expensive.

✪ They are small, so they do not take up much space.

✪ Leopard geckos are gentle and are less likely to bite than other types of geckos.

✪ They are fun to watch because of their cat-like hunting behavior.

✪ Geckos are naturally clean. They will use only one corner of their tank as a toilet.

✪ With proper care and handling, they can live for 10 to 20 years.

Leopard geckos are easy to feed. But you must not be squeamish about handling crickets and mealworms, since these are the leopard gecko's favorite food!

NOT-SO-GOOD POINTS

- ✪ Leopard geckos are fragile and need gentle handling.
- ✪ They need a constant source of warmth, such as a heat lamp.
- ✪ They need to be fed live animals (crickets, mealworms, and other insects).
- ✪ If they escape they can hide anywhere and be very difficult to catch.
- ✪ They are **nocturnal**, so you cannot expect them to be very active during the day.
- ✪ If you keep males and females together, they breed easily, so you may get more geckos than you bargained for!
- ✪ If you accidentally put male geckos together, they may fight viciously!

Yes or no?

Having a gecko for a pet means:

- giving it food and water every day
- cleaning out its tank once every two weeks
- making sure it is warm, happy, and healthy.

Are you really sure that you are prepared do all these things, even when you are in a hurry or want to do something else? If the answer is "yes," then perhaps you have just made the decision to own a gecko!

Buying your gecko

Geckos are often sold in pet stores, but you can also buy your gecko from a **reptile breeder**. Reptile breeders advertise in newspapers, on the Internet, and in reptile magazines. They usually have lots of useful information and can give you advice on setting up your gecko's home. They can also help you make plans for getting food for your gecko. Most reptile breeders work with a specific species, so you should be able to find a breeder who specializes in leopard geckos.

WHAT TO LOOK FOR

At the pet store or the reptile breeder's, look at all the geckos, but make sure that the one you take home:

- ✪ is young
- ✪ looks lively and alert
- ✪ does not look tired or sleepy
- ✪ is active and runs around easily.

TOP TIP

Ask the pet store assistant to put some crickets or mealworms in the geckos' tank. If the gecko you like runs over and catches an insect right away, you have a winner! If your gecko does not seem interested, choose another.

This gecko is alert and waiting to pounce on the cricket. It would be a good choice for a pet.

How many geckos?

In the wild, leopard geckos live in **colonies**. These are loose groups that are usually made up of one male and about five females. You may decide that you want to keep two or more geckos together. However, there are some important points to remember about having groups of geckos.

Male geckos should not be kept together. They will fight and hurt each other. If you want to have more than one gecko, it is best to get females. Ask an experienced gecko keeper to show you how to recognize the females.

If you own several geckos, try to choose ones that are about the same size. Otherwise, the larger ones might pick on the smaller ones or keep them from eating well.

If your parents or guardians are experienced gecko owners, they may decide that you can have one male with several females. But if you have a male and females, they will probably breed. Taking care of eggs and newly hatched baby geckos is a big task.

It is probably best to start with one gecko. When you are comfortable with your new pet, you can think about getting a second gecko.

Your Gecko's Home

Pet geckos should be kept in glass tanks, like the ones used for fish. But even though leopard geckos are not great climbers, your tank should still have a lid that provides plenty of ventilation to cover it. If you have a cat or dog, the tank should always be covered. A 38-liter (10-gallon) tank will be big enough for one or two geckos. If you have more than two geckos, you will need a 57-liter (15-gallon) tank, or bigger.

Your lid should snap into place over the top of the tank so your gecko cannot squeeze between the cracks and get out!

Inside the tank

Your gecko will be much more comfortable if you put a few things inside its tank. First of all, you will need some material, known as **substrate**, to line the bottom of the tank and prevent your gecko from lying on the cold glass. The gecko will walk around and lie on this material. Many things can be used for substrate, but some commonly used natural materials are pea gravel, orchid bark, and slate tiles. Some of these materials can be bought in a pet store. Substrate materials must be dust free. Do not use anything wet—leopard geckos are from dry **environments**. Also avoid anything that the gecko can swallow, such as sand.

If you use natural materials, they will have to be cleaned frequently. Artificial materials such as artificial grass, paper towels, and newspaper are easier to clean or replace, but they do not look as natural. Paper pulp substrate is sold in pet stores and makes a good material for geckos.

Food and water

Geckos need to be given live insects to eat (see page 24) and fresh water to drink every day. Young geckos that are learning to hunt will eat much better if the insects are placed in a feeding bowl where the geckos can see them, but from which they cannot escape.

The water dish should be shallow and heavy so that it cannot be tipped over when your gecko climbs into it.

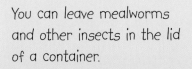
You can leave mealworms and other insects in the lid of a container.

SHELTER

It is very important to give your pet a place to rest. Your gecko will be happy with a "house" made from a small plastic container or box with a hole cut into the side, or a paper towel roll.

Making a "house" for your gecko is easy. Just ask an adult to cut a small hole in the side of a small plastic container, making sure there are no sharp edges. Put some peat moss or some **vermiculite** mixture inside the house to make it moist and cozy.

Home comforts

Just as you need a sofa and some chairs in your house, your gecko will find its home more comfortable and interesting if you add some extra things to it. Rocks that have been thoroughly cleaned and dried, and branches or hollow logs that have been properly cleaned and bought from a pet store, will imitate the gecko's environment in the wild and provide good places for your pet to climb, sleep, and take shelter.

Adding plants

There's nothing like a plant to make a house seem more like a home! Snake plants (*Sansevieria trifasciata*) and fig plants (*Ficus lyrata*) are pretty and have tough leaves that will stand up to all the trampling your gecko might do on them.

Do not stack the rocks on top of each other, as they can fall on your gecko and hurt it.

SAFETY FIRST

Always ask an experienced gecko owner which plants are safe. Some plants are poisonous to geckos.

Keeping warm

Geckos come from very warm areas of the world and need to stay warm, so your gecko will need a **heat source**. It is best to use a ceramic heater, a low-wattage red light bulb, or an under-tank heating mat to supply heat. Leopard geckos are **nocturnal**, so they do not like bright lights.

ULTRAVIOLET LIGHT

Ultraviolet light comes from the sun, and a lot of **reptiles** rely on it for their health. But leopard geckos are nocturnal, so they do not need an ultraviolet light source to stay healthy.

The daytime temperature in your gecko's tank should be between 27 and 32 °Celsius (81–89 °Fahrenheit). At night the temperature should not go below 24 °C (75 °F). Geckos like to move between different temperatures, so make sure it is warm at one end of the tank and cooler at the other. Ask an adult to help you set up the heat source and teach you how to use a thermometer.

SAFETY FIRST

Do not use heaters that look like artificial rocks. Although some people recommend these "hot rocks" as a heat source for reptiles, they are not a good idea—your gecko can burn itself on them!

This tank is heated using a low-level red light bulb. The temperature close to the bulb will be about 5 °C (40 °F) higher than the temperature at the opposite end of the tank.

Feeding Your Gecko

Geckos are fun to feed! After you have fed your gecko for a couple of weeks, it will learn when it is dinnertime. It will come out of its box to meet you when it hears you getting dinner ready, and it might even learn to eat from your hand.

Mealtimes

Because geckos are **nocturnal**, they should be fed in the evening or just before you go to bed. An adult gecko should eat once a day. A young, growing gecko should have two small meals—one in the morning and one in the evening.

What food?

You will need a constant supply of insects for your gecko. The most common insects to feed geckos are black or brown crickets, locusts, and mealworms. Wax-moth **larvae** should only be given as a treat because they contain too much fat. You can buy these insects from a pet store or order them directly through a company that specializes in **breeding** insects for feeding **reptiles**. An adult gecko should eat approximately two to five crickets a day, depending on the size of the cricket.

With a little patience, you can teach your gecko to take food from your hand. As long as they can *see* an insect moving, leopard geckos are *so* curious that they are likely to come over and investigate!

Mealworms should be available for your gecko all the time. You can watch your gecko feeding if you stay very still and quiet and use a soft light.

Homes for food

You will need a place where your crickets and other insects can live. You can use a small tank with a ventilated lid, or a plastic tub—as long as it has a tight lid and small holes to allow the insects to breathe.

KEEPING COUNT

When you feed your gecko, watch to see how many insects it eats.

✪ Give it as much food as it will eat.

✪ After 20 minutes, take out any insects your gecko has not eaten—you know how annoying insects can be!

✪ Write down how many insects you offered and how many your gecko ate.

✪ You will soon know exactly how many insects your gecko will eat at once.

The cricket home should have holes so the crickets can breathe, but make sure that your crickets cannot get out—or you will find them jumping and chirping all over your home!

Feeding the food

The crickets, mealworms, wax-moth larvae, and locusts that you buy to feed to your gecko will need food, too! Feed the crickets and locusts a good-quality insect food (available at pet stores) and give them a clean source of water every few days. You can also shred some carrots, spinach, zucchini, or other vegetables and put them in your insect tub, and in the mealworm and wax-moth larvae tubs, too. Insects love fresh vegetables.

In a pet store, crickets are not fed, so feed them a big meal before you give them to your gecko. That way, you will give your gecko a better meal.

A varied diet

In the wild, geckos eat many different **species** of insects, so it is a good idea to give your gecko a variety of food sources. (Imagine eating pizza every day of your life!) It is even fine to feed your gecko different insects at the same time.

A clean, soaked sponge on a plastic plate is the best way to give your crickets water.

Vitamins and calcium

Crickets, mealworms, and other insects do not have all the vitamins and minerals your gecko needs. In order to grow strong, geckos also need a complete reptile vitamin powder and some reptile calcium powder. You can buy these at a pet store.

It is hard to make a gecko eat a vitamin pill, so sprinkle vitamin powder and calcium powder onto the crickets or mealworms just before feeding them to your gecko.

VACATION CARE

When you go away on vacation you must:

✪ Find a friend or neighbor who likes your gecko and whom you can trust to care for your pet. Ask the person to come in every day and give your gecko water and food.

✪ Ask your friend to check the tank temperature. Show the person how to adjust the temperature if it needs to be changed.

✪ Ask your friend to look after the insects that you feed to your gecko.

✪ Leave written instructions about how much food to give, and when to feed your pet and the insects.

✪ Leave your vet's phone number in case there is an emergency.

SAFETY FIRST

Reptile vitamin powder is not intended for humans. Never eat the vitamin powder yourself.

Caring for Your Gecko

Having a pet can be a big responsibility. If you have a gecko, you will need to do some things for it very regularly.

Misting

Sometimes you will see your gecko drinking from its water dish. But to encourage your gecko to drink, you should mist it lightly with water, using a small spray bottle. Fill the bottle with clean, warm water and lightly spray your gecko every day. In the wild, geckos drink water off leaves when they feel the rain running down their bodies. So, spraying your gecko encourages it to drink. It also helps it to shed its skin.

TOP TIPS

✪ Make sure the bottle you use to mist your gecko has never contained any cleaners or chemicals before.

✪ Do not mist your gecko with cold water. It will give your pet too much of a shock.

✪ Remember to change the water in the spray bottle every day.

Your gecko will enjoy being misted. While you mist it, it might close its eyes and you might see it lick its face, drinking the water.

Shedding skin

Like all **reptiles**, geckos need to shed their skin regularly. Moisture is very important before and during the shedding process, so make sure you keep the peat moss or **vermiculite** mixture in your gecko house moist by occasionally spraying it with water. You might notice that your gecko looks dull in color just before it sheds its old skin. The new skin is often shinier and brighter than the old one. Your gecko will eat the skin it has shed.

Adult geckos shed their skin between two and four times a year. It takes a few days for the skin to come off completely.

Checking your gecko

When you lift your gecko out of its tank, take the opportunity to get a really close look at it and see if it looks healthy. A baby gecko should grow pretty fast. If it is shedding its skin every couple of weeks, it is probably growing at a good pace. It is a good idea to measure and weigh your gecko every week or so. You will need a measuring tape and a small scale that registers ounces. An adult gecko will measure between 10 and 25 centimeters (4–10 inches) in length and have a nice fat tail, but not a fat body.

You don't need to pick up your young gecko to measure it. Just place a ruler next to it every week to see how fast it is growing.

Keeping things clean

Your gecko's home will need to be cleaned regularly. By making sure that your gecko's home is clean, you will help to keep your pet healthy and happy.

Geckos make it easy

Geckos will usually only use one area of their tank as a toilet. It makes it easier if you notice where your gecko has chosen to have its toilet, as you can put paper towels or newspaper there. That way you can just pick up the paper, throw it away, and replace it every other day.

Cleaning the tank

To keep your gecko healthy, its whole tank should be cleaned out once every two weeks. It is a good idea to have a small plastic container with holes where you can put your gecko while you clean its home. Take all the contents out of the tank and clean them individually.

Remember to replace the paper towel every other day. If you have more than one gecko, you might have to do this every day.

The tank can be cleaned with a reptile-safe cleaner that is available from pet stores. Ask an adult to help you choose the right disinfectant. After using a disinfectant, rinse the tank with lots of water and let it dry before putting back the tank contents and your gecko.

Changing the water

It is very important that your gecko drinks its water from a clean dish. Make sure you empty out your gecko's water dish, rinse it clean, and refill it with fresh water every day. Otherwise your gecko may get sick.

Make sure you always wash your hands well before and after handling your gecko, and after cleaning your gecko's toilet area or tank.

TOP TIP

Make a daily checklist to keep next to your gecko's tank.

- ✪ Has my gecko been fed?
- ✪ Does it have fresh, clean water to drink?
- ✪ Has it been misted with a spray bottle?
- ✪ Is its home clean and moist?
- ✪ Is it warm enough? (Check the thermometer.)

Handling Your Gecko

Your gecko looks soft and cuddly, but imagine how big you look to a gecko. Do not be surprised if, when you try to catch it, your gecko seems frightened and runs away. This is normal. In the wild, geckos have lots of enemies—mostly larger animals and birds—trying to eat them. Their main defense is to run away as fast as they can and hide. Your gecko will need to get used to the idea that your hand is not something that might eat it or hurt it.

PICKING UP YOUR GECKO

✪ When your gecko is used to your hand in its tank, you can slowly start to touch your pet.

✪ First, try stroking your gecko with one finger. When it seems used to that, try picking it up slowly.

✪ The best way to pick up a gecko is to gently scoop it up. Place one hand above the gecko. Close your fingers around it gently. At the same time, place your other hand underneath it.

With a little patience, you can train your gecko to get used to your hand in its tank. Do not make loud noises or move very suddenly.

Keep the gecko cupped in your hands. The tiny claws on its toes might get stuck on rocks or plants, so gently ease them off.

Tail alert!

Never pick up your gecko by its tail! When a **predator** tries to grab a gecko by the tail in the wild, the gecko's normal defense is simply to leave its tail behind. That way the gecko can make a fast getaway and the predator only gets a piece of a tail. But if, by accident, the tail comes off while you are handling your gecko, do not panic—just leave the gecko in the tank. In a few weeks, your gecko will have grown a brand new tail. It may be a different color and it is likely to be shorter than the original tail.

TAIL FACTS

Although your gecko can shed its tail and still survive, tails are very important for geckos:

- ✪ They use their tail for balance.

- ✪ They store fat in their tail. If they shed their tail, geckos have to eat more to regain all the weight they have lost.

Do not worry if your gecko loses its tail by accident. Luckily, geckos can grow new tails.

Handle with care

When you are holding your pet, do not be surprised if it wriggles! It might even wriggle out of your hands and run off. It is better if you hold your gecko over a table or bed, so it does not fall to the ground. If it gets away, it will probably run and hide. Ask an adult to help you find your gecko and return it to its tank as soon as possible. If it gets covered in dust during its adventure, get rid of the dust by gently washing your gecko by misting it with your spray bottle.

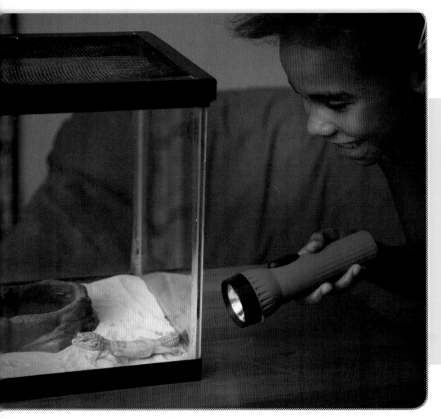

You can turn off the lights in the room and use a low-level red light or a low-power flashlight to watch your leopard gecko hunt and move around. Remember, its life starts after "lights out"!

Gecko watching

One of the best ways to enjoy your gecko is to sit and watch it while it is safe in its tank. Feeding time is always fun, and if you have more than one gecko, watching how they behave together is fascinating. So, pull up a chair and observe what your gecko does in the evening.

SAFETY FIRST

Even a healthy, clean gecko can have **bacteria** on its body that could make you sick. To avoid picking up these germs, you should always remember the following:

✪ Wash your hands with warm water and soap each time you finish handling your gecko.

✪ Do not eat while you are playing with your gecko.

✪ Do not let your gecko run across places where you put food, such as kitchen counters.

Geckos are efficient hunters. When you put an insect in the gecko's tank, the gecko will move its head to follow the insect's movements, and run after it fast!

Common Problems

Although leopard geckos are really easy to take care of, your gecko might have some problems. If you notice anything wrong, tell an adult and write down what you observed. Then ask yourself the following questions:

- When was the last time your gecko was fed?
- When was the last time it ate normally?
- When did you last see your gecko drinking?
- Is it moist in the gecko's tank? If not, spray it lightly.
- When did it last shed its skin normally?
- When was the last time your gecko looked normal?

These questions will help you to figure out how long your gecko has been sick.

No energy

If your gecko is not as active as usual, there may be a temperature problem. When geckos get cold, they do not have the energy to move around normally. Check the thermometer in your gecko's tank to make sure that the tank is warm enough. If the temperature is below 24°Celsius (75°Fahrenheit), ask an adult to help you adjust the **heat source**. Maybe the heat bulb is broken and your gecko has become cold.

If you have to take your gecko to the vet, it will be very helpful to remember all the details about when your pet became sick.

Standing in an area with high humidity can moisten your gecko's skin and help it to finish shedding normally.

When geckos get cold, they are less active than normal and may look sleepy.

Shedding problems

If you notice that your gecko is not shedding its skin properly (if parts of its old skin stay stuck to its body for more than a couple of days), gently put your gecko in a small plastic container with warm, damp paper towels on the bottom. After about 30 minutes in this moist place, the skin should loosen enough for the gecko to be able to shed it. If there is still skin hanging onto parts of your gecko's body, take your pet to a vet.

HAPPY AND HEALTHY?

✪ Is your gecko eating?

✪ Is your gecko drinking?

✪ Is your gecko's home clean?

✪ Does your gecko look healthy?

✪ Is your gecko shedding its skin normally?

✪ Is your baby gecko growing?

If the answer to all these questions is "yes," then you are probably taking good care of your gecko.

Eating problems

There are many reasons why your gecko might not eat. It may be because it is too cold, because it is sick, or because it does not like the food you are offering. If you notice that your gecko is not eating its crickets like it used to, pick it up gently and check it carefully. Sometimes geckos get tired of eating the same thing all the time. Try feeding it a different kind of insect, but also tell an adult what is happening.

If the problem continues...

If your gecko is still not eating even after you have changed its diet, and if it seems less active than usual even when the temperature is warm enough, then it may be sick. This is especially likely if your gecko does not respond to your hand or touch like it used to, if its skin looks saggy and wrinkly, or if it keeps its eyes closed a lot. Tell an adult right away and talk about making an appointment with a vet to have your pet examined.

If you are worried about your gecko, talk to an adult about taking your pet to a vet.

DON'T FORGET

Most **reptiles** can survive for days or even weeks without eating. But they cannot live without water. Make sure your gecko has clean, fresh water every day. You can encourage your gecko to drink by misting it gently with the spray bottle or by letting it stand in a shallow bath of warm water for a few minutes.

This gecko is too skinny. When a gecko loses weight, it is very important that it is examined by a vet. Geckos are so little that even losing a small amount of weight is very bad for them.

SOME OTHER PROBLEMS

Here are some other things to look out for:

- ✪ Is your gecko looking skinny? (It might be losing weight.)

- ✪ Does it have any lumps or bumps on its body?

- ✪ Is it dragging a leg? (It could have a broken leg or a sprained joint.)

- ✪ Has some of its skin turned a different color? (It could have a skin infection.)

Check your gecko's skin carefully. If the color of your gecko's skin looks **abnormal**, it may be infected. Skin infections and abnormal growth need to be treated by a vet.

Visiting the Vet

Just as you go to a doctor for checkups, your new gecko will need to visit a vet for a physical examination. But do not worry: your gecko will not need any shots unless it is sick! Soon after you buy your gecko, ask an adult to make an appointment with a vet who is used to working with **reptiles**. This will give your vet a chance to meet your gecko. The vet can also give you advice on how to care for your pet and how to recognize when it might be sick.

CHECKING YOUR PET

Your vet will want to give your gecko a thorough physical examination. During the examination the vet will probably:

- ✪ weigh your gecko
- ✪ watch your gecko from a distance to make sure it is active and lively
- ✪ look for **mites** and other skin **parasites**
- ✪ make sure the gecko is not too skinny
- ✪ open its mouth and look at its teeth and gums
- ✪ feel the gecko's belly to make sure the **organs** inside are normal
- ✪ check its legs
- ✪ listen to its heart and lungs
- ✪ check a sample of your gecko's droppings to make sure they do not contain parasites.

Your vet will examine your gecko carefully to make sure it is healthy.

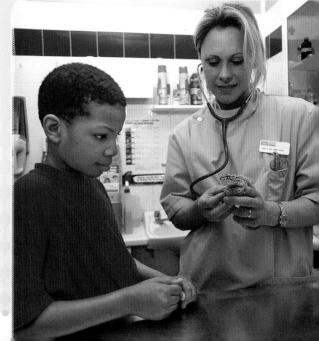

Ask your vet to tell you how much your gecko weighs and write it down, along with the date. This will *be* useful when you weigh your pet, so you can tell if it is gaining or losing weight.

Saying goodbye

Leopard geckos can live for as long as 20 years, but no matter how well you care for your pet, one day it will die. Sometimes a gecko will die peacefully and unexpectedly at home. This will come as a shock to you, but do not blame yourself. There is probably nothing you could have done.

As a caring owner, the hardest responsibility of all is to know when to let your pet be **put down** to save it from suffering. Your gecko may be very old and in pain. Or it may have a serious illness that cannot be cured. Your vet will give your gecko a small injection. This will make your pet fall asleep, and its heart will stop beating.

FEELING UPSET

No matter how it happens, you will feel upset when your gecko dies, especially if it has been a friend for many years. It is perfectly normal for people, adults as well as children, to be sad when a pet dies, or when they think of a dead pet.

Keeping a Record

Owning a leopard gecko can be a big responsibility. It is difficult to remember all the important things you need to do in order to keep your gecko healthy and happy. Making a gecko scrapbook is a good way to keep all the information handy for when you need it.

Filling your scrapbook

There are many things you can write in your scrapbook. You can start by describing your trip to the pet store or to the **reptile breeder**. You may also want to describe the first day you brought your gecko home, so you can look back later and remember how you felt and what your gecko looked like!

Write down the name you chose for your gecko. Also make a note of your gecko's weight and length when you brought it home.

When you take your gecko to the vet for its first visit, take your scrapbook along and write down what happens there. Keep important details, such as the name and phone number of your vet, in your scrapbook.

On the prowl

My two geckos together

Dinnertime

You could take fun pictures of your gecko and add them to your scrapbook. Remember to label them afterward.

Important information

Write down information about your pet in your scrapbook:

- When you start to feed your gecko, keep notes about what it eats, and how much.

- Each time you weigh and measure your gecko, write down its weight and length.

- Whenever your gecko does something unusual, write it down.

- Stick labels from vitamin powder, cricket food, and other things you use for your gecko into your scrapbook.

TOP TIP

Collect magazine articles about leopard geckos and other geckos, cut them out, and stick them in your scrapbook.

Soon you will have a complete gecko record. When you take your gecko to the vet for checkups or if it is sick, take your scrapbook. The information may be very useful.

Understanding Geckos

Geckos are very popular. Lots of people love geckos because they look so interesting and behave in such fascinating ways. Now that you have read this book, you will understand geckos and their world much better, but owning a gecko of your own will make you appreciate geckos even more. Once you have a gecko as a pet, you will want to find out more about geckos and their lives.

Sharing the fun

Many people throughout the world own geckos. It is fun and helpful to get in touch with other people who love geckos as much as you do. In fact, if you ask around at school, you may find other kids like you who have geckos as pets! Bring some pictures of your gecko to school. Draw your gecko's home or take a photo of it to show to your science teacher.

Reading books and magazines about geckos and other reptiles will help you to understand more about your pet.

Getting together with other kids who appreciate geckos can be fun. They can tell you about their experiences with their geckos, and you can share your stories, too.

NOW TRY THIS

Here are some more ways to find out about geckos:

✪ Check out your local library and bookstore. There are hundreds of books written about geckos, and many of these have very helpful information about leopard geckos.

✪ Visit zoos and nature centers. They will have fascinating **reptiles** to watch and lots of information about reptiles in the wild.

✪ With an adult, visit other gecko lovers' websites or the websites of reptile **breeders**. There you will see beautiful pictures of many types of geckos and read about their unusual lives!

✪ Go to a magazine store and find out what magazines they have about reptiles or geckos. Perhaps you will be able to buy a magazine regularly.

✪ Ask an adult to help you find a local **herpetology** group. *Herpetology* means the study of reptiles and amphibians. (Amphibians are animals that live on land and in water, such as frogs and toads.)

✪ Get in touch with a reptile breeder. Your local breeder will probably know of other kids who are interested in geckos. You can talk to them and maybe start a leopard gecko fan club!

Most zoos have a reptile house with a wide range of reptiles of different sizes.

Glossary

abnormal different from what is usual or normal

arboreal related to, or living in, trees

bacteria tiny one-celled creatures that can cause disease

bask lie in the sun and absorb its warmth

breed mate and produce young

breeder someone who owns animals and encourages them to mate and produce young

camouflage colors and markings that blend in with the surroundings

captivity under the control of humans

cold-blooded having the same body temperature as the surrounding air or water

colony group of creatures that live together

crevice narrow crack

defense mechanism automatic reaction to avoid danger

diurnal active during the day

environment surroundings and weather conditions in an area

habitat place where an animal or plant lives and grows

heat source place where warmth or heat comes from, such as the sun

herpetology study of reptiles and amphibians

larva (more than one: **larvae**) young of an insect at the stage when it has just come out of an egg and looks like a worm

mite small blood-sucking insect

nectar sweet, sugary liquid inside a flower

nocturnal active at night

organ part of the body that has a specific purpose

parasite small creature, such as a tick or worm, that lives on or in another animal

pesticide substance that kills insects or other pests that are harmful to plants

predator animal that lives by killing or eating other animals

pupil dark hole in the middle of the colored part of an eye

put down give a sick animal an injection to help it die peacefully and without pain

reptile cold-blooded animal with scaly or tough skin

species group of animals that share characteristics and can produce young together

substrate soft material put in the bottom of a gecko tank

urban sprawl area of houses and other buildings built as a town or city grows larger

vermiculite yellow or brown mineral, like soil, used to line the bottom of many pet tanks

Find Out More

Books

There are not many books on geckos written for young readers. This is a list of books about geckos written for adults:

Bartlett, Richard D., and Patricia Pope Bartlett. *Leopard and Fat Tailed Geckos*. Hauppauge, N.Y.: Barron's, 2009.

Indiviglio, Frank. *Leopard Gecko*. Hoboken, N.J.: Wiley, 2007.

Palika, Liz. *Leopard Geckos for Dummies*. Hoboken, N.J.: Wiley, 2007.

Websites

www.leopardgeckoguide.com
This website gives advice about how to care for geckos.

www.geckocare.net
This is a useful website offering gecko facts and advice about how to care for your pet.

www.officialusa.com/stateguides/zoos
This website provides details on zoos in the United States, which you might want to visit to learn more about geckos and other reptiles.

Index

baby geckos 5, 9, 11, 14, 15, 19, 29
basking 6
bites 11
breeding 14, 17, 19
buying your gecko 10, 18

calcium powder 27
camouflage 9
climbing 4, 5, 9, 11
colors and markings 9, 12
crickets 17, 18, 24, 25, 26

daily checklist 31
death 41

eating problems 38
eggs 5, 9, 14, 15, 19
eyelids 5, 8, 11, 13
eyes 5, 8

female geckos 9, 14, 15, 19
fighting 17, 19
finding out about geckos 44, 45, 47
food 5, 6, 7, 8, 13, 17, 18, 21, 24–27, 38

gecko species 6–7, 10, 11
gecko watching 34–35

habitats 6–7
handling geckos 11, 32–35
health care 36–41
heat source 23, 36
herpetology 45
"house" 21–22
hunting 6, 17, 21, 34, 35

infections 39
insect tub 25, 26

legal facts 10
length 8, 12, 29, 43
leopard geckos 11–19
life span 16, 41
lizards 4
lumps and bumps 39

male geckos 14, 17, 19
mating 14
mealworms 17, 18, 21, 24, 26
misting 28, 34, 38
mites 40

nocturnal habits 8, 17, 23, 24
noises 4, 5

owning groups of geckos 19

parasites 40
plants 22
predators 11, 12, 32, 33
pupils 8

reptile breeders 18, 45
reptiles 4

safety 22, 23, 27, 35
scales 4, 12
scrapbook 42–43
size 8, 12, 29
skin 4, 12, 39
skin infections 39
skin, shedding 29, 37
substrate 20

tail 4, 5, 29, 33
tail vibration 14
tank cleaning 17, 20, 30
tanks 20–23
teeth and gums 40
temperatures 23, 36
threat to geckos 7
toe pads 4, 5, 9, 13
toilet habits 16, 30
Tokay gecko 8, 11
tongue 5, 8

ultraviolet light 23

vacation care 27
vets 36, 38, 40
vitamin powder 27

wall geckos 6
warmth 17, 23, 36
water 21, 28, 31, 38
weight 12, 29, 33, 39, 41, 43
wild, geckos in the 12–13, 14, 15, 19

zoos 45